The story of the National Wallace Monument

Ranald MacInnes

Someone Publishing Ltd

• William Wallace by George Jamesone, 1633.
Stirling Smith Art Gallery & Museum.

'Ah, freedome is a noble thing'

John Barbour, 1375

The enduring power of freedom

The National Wallace Monument is one of Scotland's most celebrated landmarks. The stunning 67 metre tower honours a national hero who gave his life for his country. The monument took eight years to build, and was funded entirely by contributions from the public totalling more than £15,000. 80,000 people made their way to the town of Stirling from all over Scotland and beyond to attend the ceremony of the laying of the foundation stone.

This instantly recognisable icon, rising from the beautiful wooded slopes of the Abbey Craig near Stirling, is visited by more than 100,000 people every year - a testament to the enduring power of freedom. Here we tell the story behind the building of Scotland's most important monument.

· The National Wallace Monument on the Abbey Craig against the backdrop of the Ochils

• William Wallace by an unknown 19th century artist.
Stirling Smith Art Gallery & Museum.

'Never-conquered Scots'

Scotland's precious freedom is as old as the country itself and at the heart of the nation's story is the idea of the 'never-conquered Scots'. Although for many centuries hostile neighbours, Scotland and England were independent kingdoms. However, from the 13th century it was grandly assumed by English monarchs that they would overpower and rule the whole of the British Isles. But this was to reckon without Scottish resistance. Overlordship of Scotland, as achieved by Edward I in Wales, was never accepted politically and never accomplished militarily. Later Scottish historians basked in Wallace's glory and traced a line of rulers improbably back to Scota, the daughter of an Egyptian pharaoh. Over these thousands of years, they argued, Scotland had never been conquered, and a range of invaders, including the Romans, had been repelled. The most momentous of the many defeats inflicted on would-be invaders was masterminded by Scotland's oldest and most revered national hero, Sir William Wallace, who saved Scotland at a time of grave national emergency in 1297. Wallace's heroic actions spurred the country on to resist English oppression and so settle Scotland's independence.

• Edward I, King of England (r. 1272 - 1307).

The Lion & the Unicorn.

By the middle of the 19th century, the events of Wallace's illustrious life were long ago but not forgotten. They had been remembered in countless tales and traditions. However, it was assumed by many after the Union of Crowns in 1603 and the Union of Parliaments in 1707 that Scotland and England would eventually merge into one nation. In the years of prosperity of the early 19th century, a movement began to bring together the two countries legally, administratively and culturally. It was in this context that the cult of Scotland's champion, William Wallace, was taken up as the symbol of a new political message. When it seemed that Scotland might at last be swallowed up by its larger partner, the country's ancient independence was again stressed through an astonishing 'Wallace revival'. This time, however, it was not separation that was demanded but equality *within* the Union: recognition of Scotland's status as an equal partner with England. The name of Wallace was invoked to champion Scotland's right to a fair political share of the United Kingdom and the British Empire.

• In this print of 1818, the lion of England is shown fighting over the Crown with the Scottish unicorn. The official Royal Coat of Arms has the two beasts arranged in harmony. Scotland is also often portrayed as a lion, as in Noel Paton's design for the National Wallace Monument (page 24).

Wilhelnus Walius, Scoteus, et de Scotia ortus

(William Wallace, a Scot and of Scottish birth) Indictment, Westminster, 23 August 1305

• Image of Mel Gibson as Wallace from the film *Braveheart*.

Historians cannot agree over the facts of William Wallace's biography and, inevitably, much of his eventful life has been embroidered, as happens to all heroes. The 1995 film *Braveheart* was only one re-telling of the tale according to the fashion of the day. We know of several key events of Wallace's life in detail, but not the exact circumstances of the patriot's birth. Wallace seems to have been born around 1270, either at Elderslie near Paisley or Ellerslie in Ayrshire, into a minor noble family. But if the circumstances of Wallace's birth are sketchy, those of his death are all too clear in their awful details. William Wallace was tried by a court he refused to recognise, found guilty, hanged, disembowelled, beheaded and quartered in 1305 as a 'rebel' at Smithfield in London.

The charges against Wallace and the typically barbaric death sentence imposed are well documented. He suffered the same fate as the Welsh leader Dafydd ap Gruffudd who, 22 years before, had also risen up against English occupation of his country. However, Wallace's death was not the end of Scotland's independence, but the beginning. Robert the Bruce was to take up the challenge laid down by Wallace and see it through to the momentous victory of Bannockburn in 1314.

• William Wallace is tried before Edward I at Westminister Hall after a painting by Daniel Maclise.

Alexander III
King of Scotland
(r. 1249 - 1286).

Margaret
'Maid of Norway'
(r. 1286 - 1290)
From a frieze by William Hole
in the Scottish National
Portrait Gallery.

Robert the Bruce
King of Scotland
(r. 1306 - 1329)
Bruce had a strong claim to the
Crown through his great grandfather
David I of Scotland.

From 1286, following the death of King Alexander III of Scotland, the country came very close to being conquered and ruled by England. Alexander's heir was his grandchild Margaret, the infant daughter of the King of Norway. The English King Edward had suggested that Margaret should marry his son, also Edward, and this was ratified in the Treaty of Birgham (1290). Under the terms of the treaty, Scotland was to remain an independent kingdom, but when the 'Maid of Norway' tragically died on the journey to Scotland, the succession was thrown open to several claimants, the strongest of whom were John Balliol and Robert the Bruce. Edward I seized the opportunity presented by doubts over the succession and appointed a 'puppet king', John Balliol. When Balliol proved less of a puppet than Edward wished, the English king invaded Scotland, destroying its heritage and removing to England the stone of destiny, on which Scottish monarchs had been crowned for centuries. Edward then installed a whole layer of English administrators: sheriffs, bailies and 'alkyn other officeris' to run the country. The brutal military occupation that followed stoked the fires of nationalist sentiment in Scotland and, following the killing of the English sheriff Hazelrig at Lanark, William Wallace placed himself at the head of an armed national resistance along with another lesser known but equally brilliant Scottish commander, Andrew de Moray.

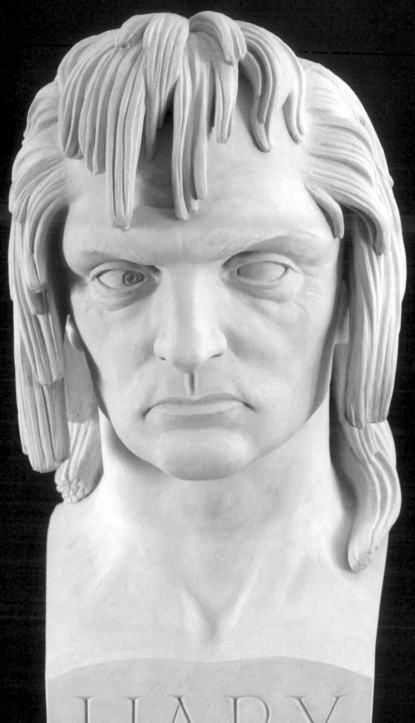

HARY

QVHAM THOWIS
THOW SCOT

*'Many brave men lived before Agamemnon;
but all are overwhelmed in eternal night,
because they lack a sacred poet.'*

Horace (65 BC - 8 BC), Odes

Blind Harry

Much of the story of Wallace is known to us through the late 15th century poem by Henry the Minstrel (known as Blind Harry). Very little is known of the details of Blind Harry's life. Probably blind from birth, he was born into a noble family and is credited with writing the patriotic epic, *The Life and Heroic Actions of the Renowned Sir William Wallace, General and Governor of Scotland*, around 1460. Although this work is the main source of information on Wallace's life it has been shown to contain many errors of fact having been written 160 years after Wallace's death. There is also some doubt that this huge, 12-volume work could have been written by one man. Nevertheless as a piece of literature the work is of immense value and contains a wealth of information about life in the time of Wallace.

· James III, King of Scotland (r. 1460 - 1488).

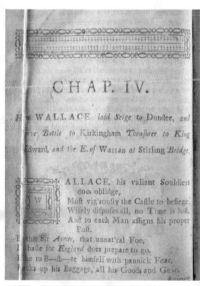

· 1723 edition of the poem by Blind Harry translated from Scots by Sir William Hamilton of Gilbertfield.

The only surviving text of Blind Harry's epic poem is contained in a manuscript held by the National Library of Scotland, written out in 1488 by John Ramsay, who also copied for posterity *The Bruce* by John Barbour (c. 1316 - 1395). Originally, the poem would have undoubtedly been read aloud in a series of performances before its patron, King James III, and other persons of high rank. Between 1473 and 1492, Blind Harry is recorded as being paid for performances as a minstrel at James's court in Linlithgow Palace. He may also have written several other poems which have not survived. In 1723 Sir William Hamilton of Gilbertfield re-issued Blind Harry's epic account of Wallace's life in a modern form. Next to the Bible, Hamilton's text became the most widely owned book in Scotland and inspired Robert Burns' famous battle hymn *Scots Wha Hae*.

· Blind Harry bust by Alexander Stoddart, 1996.
Stirling Smith Art Gallery & Museum.

The Battle of Stirling Bridge

'For this reason the Scots adopted a stout heart at the instigation of William Wallace, who taught them to fight, so that those whom the English nation held as living captives might be made renewed Scots in their own homeland. Hence in the year one thousand three hundred less three times one the Scots vanquished the English, whom they put into mourning for death, as the bridge bears witness, where the great battle is recorded, which lies beyond Stirling on the River Forth'

Walter Bower *Scotichronicon* (c. 1385 - 1449)

In September 1297, four months after Wallace's rising began, John de Warenne, earl of Surrey, marched north on Edward's instructions. With a huge force of heavy cavalry and infantry, he was confident of victory. The town of Stirling was the main entry point to the north of Scotland, its bridge regarded as the strategic key to the whole country. The Scots were encamped just north of Stirling Bridge on the Abbey Craig, where the National Wallace Monument stands today. Their army was predominantly infantry, armed with long spears, and drawn mainly from the 'lesser' ranks of society, as many of the nobility were being held captive in England.

• Postcard image of the Battle of Stirling Bridge by Robert William Brown. This was a major watercolour painting which hung in the National Wallace Monument until the 1940s. It was in poor condition at that time and was probably discarded. Stirling Smith Art Gallery & Museum.

The Wallace Coat of Arms.

Coat of Arms of
Andrew de Moray.

Coat of Arms of
John de Warenne, earl of Surrey.

From the base of the Abbey Craig a causeway stretched for over a kilometre across the River Forth's flood plain. At its end stood the bridge (lying 180 metres upstream from the 15th century stone bridge that still crosses the river today). Wide enough for only two horsemen to pass abreast, the bridge would have taken several hours to cross. And even having reached their goal, the English army could only enter a confined loop in the river, leaving their flank exposed to attack. Wallace and his fellow commander Moray banked on this turn of events. The Scottish army had taken up a position on the other side of the river but Warenne decided to delay and pursue a negotiated settlement, demanding complete surrender in exchange for peace where Wallace wanted withdrawal of the English forces. There was no middle ground.

As day dawned on 11 September 1297, the English and Welsh infantry started to cross the bridge, only to be recalled because their leader, Warenne, had overslept. Turning back and re-grouping, the infantry crossed again but were recalled once more. Warenne had received false intelligence that the Scots wanted to negotiate. He sent two Dominican friars to accept the terms of Wallace's surrender but they came back with a hostile statement, the first such record of Wallace's words:

'Tell your commander that we are not here to make peace but to do battle, defend ourselves and liberate our kingdom. Let them come on, and we shall prove this in their very beards.'

The trap is sprung

With Wallace unrepentant and ready to do battle, the English had no option but to proceed with the crossing of Stirling Bridge. Such a crossing by exposed infantrymen and cavalry was what Wallace and Moray had been hoping for. They waited until more than half of the English had made the crossing before springing their trap. Scots spearmen charged down the causeway. Those on the right flank forced their way along the river bank to the north end of the bridge, cutting off any hope of escape. Trapped in a confined space, the English cavalry was heavy and immobile. Only one group of English knights, under Sir Marmaduke de Thweng, succeeded in forcing its way back to the bridge, and safety. Warenne, who remained on the south bank of the river, ordered the bridge to be destroyed and retreated with the remains of his army to Berwick. Another telling of the story has it that a local carpenter, nicknamed 'Pin' Wright, had been hidden under the bridge and at the crucial moment pulled a pin to bring the structure crashing down into the river.

19th century Burgh of Stirling wax seal depicting the Battle of Stirling Bridge. Stirling Smith Art Gallery & Museum.

• Battle of Stirling Bridge, 11 September 1297, from Cassell's *History of England*.

* Battle of Stirling Bridge from a frieze by William Hole in the Scottish National Portrait Gallery.

With no way forward or back, more than half of the mighty English war machine was left stranded on the north side of the river Forth. More than 100 men-at-arms and 5,000 Welsh infantry were caught and slaughtered by the Scottish forces, including the greatest prize, Hugh de Cressingham, Edward's 'fat and comely' tax collector. A grisly tradition has it that Wallace had a sword-belt made from the hated official's skin. The most severe loss for the Scots was that of Wallace's co-leader, the brilliant tactician Andrew de Moray, who was wounded in the battle and died two months later.

Victory brought an immediate end to English occupation and Wallace, now titled and accepted by the aristocracy as Guardian of Scotland, went on to lay waste to the north of England in the hope of forcing Edward to acknowledge the power of the Scots. The cycle of killing and burning, initiated by Edward's sack of Berwick on 30 March 1296, continued.

A turning point

The Battle of Stirling Bridge was a hugely important turning point not only in Scotland's history but also in medieval battle. It has been described as marking 'the end of the Middle Ages'. Until 1297 the heavily armed and mounted knight had been unstoppable, but at Stirling Bridge a common army of enlisted spearmen defeated feudal knights in full armour. This may have ushered in the beginning of modern warfare: only five years later, a host of French knights was destroyed by spear-wielding Flemish townsmen at The Battle of Courtrai. The Battle of Stirling Bridge also destroyed the myth of English invincibility. The Scots had not defeated a major English army since the Dark Ages, but this victory strengthened their will to resist Edward I. However, losing to the Scots also strengthened Edward's will to triumph: less than a year later Wallace's army was defeated at the Battle of Falkirk (1298).

At Falkirk a more traditional pitched battle took place. The English cavalry had a clear run and the archers (many of whom had been recruited in Wales following that country's virtual annexation less than 20 years before) inflicted heavy damage on the massed ranks of the Scots. Falkirk was a huge blow for Wallace who never again commanded an army. However, the seeds of resistance had been sown and bore fruit in the spectacularly successful campaign of Robert the Bruce, who finally established Scotland's independence on the battlefield of Bannockburn in 1314.

William Wallace over the body of Cressingham, painted by David Scott, 1843. Paisley Art Gallery & Museum.

Robert the Bruce: equestrian statue at the site of his victory at Bannockburn, by Pilkington Jackson, 1964.

Heroes and hero worship

'Wallace's heroic patriotism as conspicuous in his death as in his life so roused and inspired his country that within nine years of his betrayal the work of his life was crowned with victory and Scotland's independence gained on the field of Bannockburn'

• Painting of the Battle of Bannockburn, 24 June 1314, by Mark Churms, 1994.

These words, inscribed on the monument of 1900 near Glasgow at the scene of Wallace's betrayal by the earl of Menteith, sum up the cult of Wallace. It is a form of national worship which is rivalled only by that of Robert the Bruce or, in literature, Robert Burns, who popularised the modern Wallace and Bruce cult with his great hymn of praise to the two patriots, *Scots Wha Hae* (Scots who have…with Wallace bled). The cult of Wallace has been continuous, but it reached its highest architectural point at the Abbey Craig in Stirling where the astonishing monument still commands the flat terrain below, including the victorious sites of Stirling Bridge and Bannockburn.

• Plaque at the Wallace Monument, Robroyston, Glasgow, 1900.

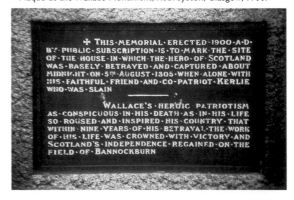

∘ Hungarian national hero, Arpad, from the gigantic painting by Arpad Fetzy.

∘ William Tell Monument,
Altdorf, Switzerland.

Every nation has its historical heroes: Arpad of Hungary, William Tell of Switzerland and many others. Some of these figures have been 'liberators', their role to personify the nation or to act as a symbolic father. Great deeds and heroic attributes cluster around the hero and they become almost god-like. Indeed, Wallace's martyrdom at the hands of the English has a Christ-like narrative, the prisoner bound in chains and ironically crowned with a victory laurel. The cult of Wallace was traditionally celebrated by kings and commoners, in folklore but also in the high art of literature. However, in the late 18th and early 19th centuries, the cult took on a new, dynamic meaning, related closely to Scotland's place in the 'New Britain'. Wallace could now stand for the country's grievances, but his cult could also accommodate a more radical or even a religious dimension. The freedom with which Wallace was associated had almost infinite potential. Wallace has even been portrayed as the defender of ancient British freedom from the 'Norman yoke' of Edward and the Plantagenets.

A symbol of nationhood

The cult of Wallace resulted in a series of ever more grandiose and ambitious monuments being erected in his honour. The movement reached an astonishing fever pitch in the mid-19th century. This was the epoch of the monument: a time of innumerable statues and buildings raised to martyrs and heroes. The fact that there are more than 20 Wallace monuments throughout the country should not come as a surprise, but their scale is quite remarkable: from Thomas Hamilton's tower at Ayr to the sculpted Iona cross at Robroyston in Glasgow. Looking at these monuments we can also trace a developing idea of 'Scottishness' in architecture.

The first large monument to William Wallace was at Dryburgh in the Scottish Borders. This was the brainchild of the nationalist earl of Buchan, who paid for the colossal statue himself. Next came the idea of a *building* as monument: the Wallace tower at Ayr (1833) introduced the idea of planning a monument set in an urban context, which, of course, was developed at Edinburgh's Scott Monument (1844).

• Wallace Monument, Dryburgh, 1814.

• Wallace Tower, Ayr.

· Glasgow Tolbooth, prior to demolition of the main block.

· King's College, Aberdeen.

· St Giles' Cathedral, Edinburgh.

The ultimate Wallace monument is, of course, the National Wallace Monument at the Abbey Craig in Stirling, designed by the Edinburgh-born Glasgow architect J. T. Rochead and built between 1861 and 1869. It is a massive tower, set on a hill and growing out of a thick forest, dominating the landscape for many miles around. The monument's essential elements - the symbols of its Scottishness - now reached their full maturity: its form, a great tower with extruded stair turret; its material, roughly hewn stone; its skyline feature, a crown spire; and its massive bronze sculpture. The design is intentionally 'national': the tower with its gatehouse and the crown spire, a peculiarly Scottish motif. Adapted from St Giles' Cathedral in Edinburgh, King's College in Aberdeen and Glasgow's Tolbooth, the crown spire derives from James III's imperial emblem of authority. However, the idea of mixing these two elements in one design was absolutely original and initiated a series of crown spire church compositions in the later 19th century, including one by Rochead's critic, J. J. Stevenson, at Belmont Parish Church, Glasgow.

A public devotion

Prior to 1850 many people in Scotland had consciously attempted to assimilate themselves into a single British culture and this meant blurring the distinction between the two countries. There had been an uneasy relationship between the idea of Scottish nationhood and that of progress. Wallace had been celebrated in countless paintings in middle-class households but the cult was set to break out into a more ostentatious form. 'Old' no longer had to mean 'old-fashioned' and the scene was set for a much more public devotion to the nation's past.

The first association between Scottish ruggedness of construction and the symbolism of nationhood occurred at the National Wallace Monument and this led ultimately to an astonishing outpouring of ever more fantastic Baronial monuments. The end of the line was reached at the £250,000 (£15 million today) scheme to convert the ancient remains of Eilean Donan Castle (from 1913 - 1932) into a huge romantic complex. The idea of the castle in the landscape as a symbol of Scotland was well and truly established.

Eilean Donan Castle.

The National Wallace Monument had made
the vital connection between a rugged,
castle-like monumentalism and an idea
of 'Scottishness' which we take for granted
today. But such a connection was by no
means accepted in the earlier part of the
19th century. Ruined castles in the landscape
were often referred to as 'Wallace' towers but
the idea behind the monument demanded
first the rediscovery of the national
architecture, from the time before the
17th century. From here it was a short step
to placing the historical figure of Wallace
in a setting perceived as appropriate,
a revived form of one of the early castles
of Scotland. As a tower house or castle
the building would not only fit into the
landscape as a familiar sight, but would
also make a connection in the mind
of the public with the historic times
of Wallace's life.

Drawing of the National Wallace Monument. During the construction many prints
such as this were produced for fundraising.

Competition and controversy

The desire to create a truly national Wallace monument, one that would be venerated by all of Scotland, grew so great by the middle of the 19th century that it could no longer be ignored. Of course, this strong popular desire to commemorate William Wallace did not suddenly come to life in 1860. An abiding memory of Wallace as a national champion had been kept alive through the centuries in tales and traditions. However, in a world where folk memory and belonging were torn apart by industrialisation, obelisks and statues began to replace memory and tradition as the medium for history and sentiment. The new way of celebrating and recording heroes was through sculpture and monuments. The classical idea of public statues was revived and socially broadened to include society's new achievers - mill owners, missionaries, novelists and, for the first time, historical figures.

Statue of David Livingstone, Scottish missionary and explorer (1813 - 1873) Kensington, London.

During the 19th century, the idea that a public figure needed a public monument gained momentum. Wellington, Lord Nelson, and the battles of Waterloo and Trafalgar had been celebrated in stone throughout the British Isles, but the death of Prince Albert in 1861 saw the memorial count reach incredible new levels. Hundreds of monuments, including the elaborate Gothic canopy of the Albert Memorial (1872 - 1876) in Kensington Gardens, London, were built to commemorate the prince consort. Along with the idea of public sculpture came the notion that such monuments could inform, educate and inspire morally uplifting thoughts in the population. The only doubts about the National Wallace Monument centred around just what thoughts such a memorial might inspire

Although the first of the Scottish-British heroes, Sir Walter Scott, had been remembered with a huge monument in Edinburgh, Wallace was quite different. He was a historical figure who meant different things to different people. And he had been, after all, an enemy of England.

• Scott Monument, Edinburgh.

• Albert Memorial, London.

• Nelson's Column, Trafalgar Square, London.

What is it to be?

* Noel Paton's design for the National Wallace Monument, 1856.
Stirling Smith Art Gallery & Museum.

From the start, there were objections that veneration of Wallace was a 'sleeping dog that should be let lie'. This was dismissed as 'an absurdity' by the proposers of the monument but the anti-English problem remained, and even grew more intense. By the time a committee had chosen the first preferred design by Noel Paton, feelings were running dangerously high. Paton produced a provocative design: a Scottish lion in the act of killing the English typhon, a mythical beast. The issue continued to rankle before, during, and after the monument's completion. Efforts were made to play down the problem. At the mass meeting to inaugurate the campaign to finance the monument, held on 24 June 1856 at King's Park, Stirling, the anniversary of the Battle of Bannockburn, Sheriff Bell of Glasgow reminded the crowds that 'Scotland and England are now one' and that 'Any Scotchman who entertains animosity towards England, and any Englishman who entertains animosity towards Scotland may be set down as simply insane'.

• Statue of Liberty, New York.

• Scott Monument, George Square, Glasgow.

Further objections to the idea of a monument were on the basis that Wallace's memory lived on 'in the hearts of the people' and therefore did not require a physical memorial. It was countered after the death in 1861 of Prince Albert that such a sentiment was an insult to the prince consort whose memorials were springing up all over the country.

Then there was the form of the monument. The first design had been rejected on the grounds of anti-Englishness but what type of monument *should* it be? Monuments were varied but they split broadly into three groups in the 19th century: the 'colossus', which developed spectacularly into examples like the Statue of Liberty or Soviet monuments, the canopied shrine, which has its 19th century origins in the Scott Monument in Edinburgh and is seen at the Albert Memorial in London, and finally the column and statue seen at the Nelson Monument in Trafalgar Square, London or the Scott Monument in George Square, Glasgow. A colossus was at first preferred by Charles Rogers, the influential secretary of the building committee. He argued in 1851 that a 'colossal statue of the national hero…would be particularly suitable for the summit of Abbey Craig', even if William Stirling of Keir (whose house overlooked the Craig) disagreed strongly. It is interesting to imagine for a moment how such a statue might look today. A memory of the idea exists in the addition of a 4 metre statue of Wallace, placed on the monument in 1887, but imagine this at 30 metres, seen in silhouette on the hill.

So why was Stirling chosen as the location? The idea for a national monument went back as far as 1818 but it was to take another 50 years to realise the project. The original idea had been to put up a monument in Glasgow but this had 'excited jealousy in the city's eastern rival', Edinburgh, and eventually the compromise of Stirling was agreed.

'A tall and stately tower'

In common with many prestige projects, the decision was made to set up a new architectural competition for the monument, a relatively recent idea initiated for the building of the Palace of Westminster in 1832. There were 106 entries but only two are known to have survived: the winning design itself and a rather static design by the firm of Peddie and Kinnear which won second premium. Peddie and Kinnear were one of the most successful exponents of Scottish Baronial architecture and had designed an entire street in Edinburgh in that style.

But what of the other entries? The only description we have is in a letter by William Stirling of Keir who saw 16 designs and complained loudly about them to the convener of the National Wallace Monument Committee. In his letter, Keir worried that the Abbey Craig would be spoiled by 'well-meaning Wallace worshippers' and thought that none of the designs submitted was suitable for the site. These included what Keir described as a 'mahogany colonnade', a 'round tower with three gilt galleries like the minaret of a mosque', a 'telescopic' tower, 'an indescribable conglomeration of classical columns and ornament', and a 'poor imitation of the Edinburgh Scott Monument'. Keir's own description of an appropriate design comes remarkably close to what was eventually chosen by the committee: 'A tall and stately tower, of our early national architecture… A statue of the hero might be introduced in a niche in the southern front, or at one of the southern angles. On the north side a spacious screw staircase would form a fine architectural feature.'

· Peddie and Kinnear's design for the National Wallace Monument competition. Their anonymous entry was labelled *Liberty*.

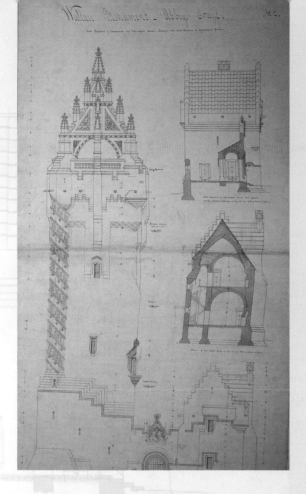

Marble bust of Rev. Charles Rogers
(1825 - 1890), by D. W. Stevenson, 1892.
Rogers was secretary of the
National Wallace Monument
building committee.

J. T. Rochead's winning design, elevations, section and (below) plan.

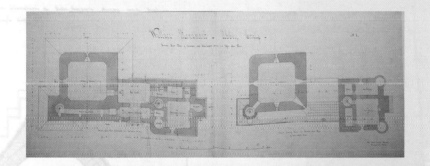

Marble bust of William Burns
(1809 - 1876), by D. W. Stevenson, 1900.
Burns took over the National Wallace Monument
project and saw it through to completion.

The committee gave a first prize to the entry anonymously signed 'nothing on earth remains but fame'. However, the controversy raged on after the choosing of the winning design and did not end with the opening of the monument. Charles Rogers, the secretary of the building committee, seemed to be taking all the credit for the successful scheme, and this enraged the powerful Glasgow faction, William Burns and Colin Rae-Brown. In October 1877 Brown stated that 'from beginning to end the National Wallace Monument was a purely Glasgow enterprise'. And it did not end there. In August 1892, he accused Rogers of tampering with the funds for the monument. Rogers had earlier lost a libel action against Brown for defamation of character in making similar claims and had been forced to resign from his post as secretary of the fundraising committee in 1861. Rogers had gone on to amaze his former employers by continuing to collect funds through a 'supplemental committee' - funds that never, according to Brown, found their way to the project. Although by 1892 this was well in the past, the cause of Brown's great anger was the unveiling of a statue of Rogers, which had been placed in the entrance hall of the monument. Brown's continued campaign against Rogers led to the placing of a complementary statue to his rival William Burns. The two portrait busts stare resolutely forward in the monument's entrance hall.

J. T. Rochead, Architect

J. T. Rochead was born in Edinburgh in 1814. He became a pupil of the Baronial specialist David Bryce but left before that style had fully matured to work in Doncaster as a draughtsman with the firm of Hurst and Moffat. He then returned to Scotland, this time to the booming city of Glasgow to work in the firm of David and James Hamilton, then the most important practice in the city. By 1841, Rochead was practising on his own, encouraged by winning an 1840 competition for Belfast Catholic Cathedral (which was not built) and by his part in the influential design of the Western Club in Buchanan Street, Glasgow. Rochead is well known for his role in the creation of Great Western Road, Glasgow. In the late 1840s and 50s, he contributed four stately terrace designs, including the beautiful Venetian-inspired Grosvenor Terrace and, well set back, Northpark House, the palatial villa of celebrated potters the Bell brothers.

Rochead also designed Baronial public buildings and villas, but despite the coup of victory in the National Wallace Monument competition, this was not his most successful style. Indeed a villa at Dumbarton for the shipbuilder Peter Denny was satirised as an absurdity in the novel *Hatter's Castle* by A. J. Cronin. Clearly a patriotic man, Rochead served as a captain in one of the many volunteer militias and marched in uniform to the opening of the National Wallace Monument.

Rochead was a successful designer of churches, particularly in the west of Scotland and it is perhaps this type of composition, especially the imposing tower of Park Church, Glasgow, which relates architecturally to the National Wallace Monument. The conceit of placing a Scottish imperial crown, only otherwise seen on churches, on top of a castle-like structure won him the competition and led to the creation of one of the world's most potent architectural symbols.

Rochead designed the temporary Royal Arch
in Dundee, erected to commemorate
Queen Victoria's first visit to Dundee in 1884.

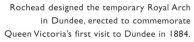

· J. T. Rochead (1814 - 1878) architect of the National Wallace Monument.
Stirling Smith Art Gallery & Museum.

Work begins

The foundation stone of the National Wallace Monument was laid with due
ceremony on 24 June 1861 and the event was attended by a massive
crowd, variously estimated between 40,000 and 80,000. Initial building
went on until the summer of 1863, by which time the contractor had been
paid £3,700 towards the construction of a tower which was still only
22 metres high. The contractor was dismissed as it was realised that the
available money was not enough to complete the project. Meanwhile,
the secretary of the building committee had been removed from office.
It was at this point that William Burns, a writer, dynamic Glasgow
patriot and 'fixer', joined the committee as its convenor (chairman) and
John McLean was appointed superintendent. From the quarrying, dressing
and transporting of the stone to its painstaking construction and eventual
fitting out, the creation of the National Wallace Monument was a slow
and difficult enterprise. As fraught with difficulty as it was, choosing the

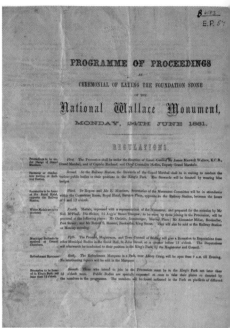

Programme of proceedings for the laying
of the foundation stone ceremony for the
National Wallace Monument, 24 June 1861
(Bannockburn Day).
Stirling Smith Art Gallery & Museum.

design proved to be the easiest part of the whole project. A sub-committee was appointed to take the work forward
to completion but immediately there were problems. At its very first meeting Rochead gave his estimate for the cost
as £5,000. However, between this date and the monument's opening, the final cost soared to £13,401. Nevertheless,
the subscription was open-ended and fundraising could carry on until completion. The project continued despite
the announcement by *The Times* as early as December 1856 that the whole thing had been 'a failure', having
by that date raised only £200.

William Burns, who campaigned for greater rights for Scotland within the
United Kingdom and became convenor of the National Wallace Monument
committee during its construction.

As building work progressed there was widespread
hostility and contempt for the monument, mostly
emanating from the English press but including
The Scotsman newspaper. However, this only spurred
the organisers on to their final goal and they boldly
began a first phase of construction, unsure of where
the money would be found to complete the project.

Just like the castles of old

The plan of the monument was at first staked out on the hill, the foundations cut and laid. In line with normal practice, as seen in an early photograph of the Scott Monument under construction, a wooden tower was probably constructed against the monument as it rose. Scaffolding a whole building for construction is a relatively modern necessity connected with improved site safety. The entire tower of the Wallace Monument was built before the linked keeper's house was even begun.

The structure's huge individual stones and the mortar had to be lifted a considerable height before the work of laying the stones and setting the vaults could even begin. These were the basic building materials, chosen for their durability. Just like the castles of old, it was argued, the monument would stand without the continual maintenance of painting or rendering.

Stone for the monument was quarried on the site at the top and the bottom of the Abbey Craig and a special railway or 'wagon way' laid to take the materials up the hill. This practice followed the original idea of 1818, but the reason behind this choice was primarily practical.

The monument's location was, of course, flexible so the strategy was to choose a site where a stone quarry was already available. The original brief of 1818 was for 'a lofty circular tower of unhewn whinstone quarried from the rock on which it is proposed to be erected. It will have a spiral staircase so that visitors may enjoy the lovely and extensive prospect to be obtained from its summit'. The first brief was based on such buildings as the Waterloo monuments of the day or the memorial to the fallen clansmen of the 1745 Jacobite Uprising, built in 1815 at Glenfinnan. The suitability of the Abbey Craig site was the one thing universally agreed upon.

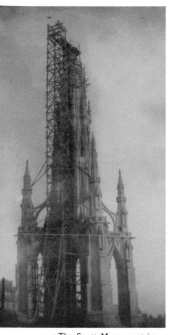

* The Scott Monument in Edinburgh with the wooden construction tower shortly before the capstone was placed in 1844.

* Glenfinnan Monument with Loch Shiel in the distance. It marks the spot where Bonnie Prince Charlie first raised his standard and was erected to commemorate the fallen clansmen of the 1745 uprising.

The original 1818 monument had been planned for Glasgow Green. Fir Park, in the north of Glasgow, was also suggested, possibly on the site of the John Knox statue erected there in 1825. Other suggestions had included Calton Hill in Edinburgh, and a Statue of Liberty-type proposition from John Steill (the donor for the Aberdeen Wallace monument), who suggested a west coast location where the monument would be 'the last object that the emigrant may set his eyes on when he leaves Scotia's shores'.

However by 1856 the Abbey Craig was widely regarded as the most suitable site, not least because it had a quarry of freestone (easily workable sandstone) at the base of the hill and also a nearby quarry of the hard whinstone used for more utilitarian, constructional work, but also because it overlooked the site of Wallace's celebrated victory at the Battle of Stirling Bridge in 1297.

• Stone masons working on the Scott Monument. Local stone was one of the benefits of the Abbey Craig site.

• View of Calton Hill from Salisbury Crags in Edinburgh, one of the sites considered for the monument.

Until the 1820s in Scotland, most building stone had been hauled very short distances to the site of construction but advances in roads and transport, including railways and canals, meant that stone could be selected and transported. However, the added cost of such a strategy would have been hard to bear or to justify. The idea of site quarrying also meshed with the medieval character of the monument. The original castles that provided a model for the monument had been built from stones quarried virtually on site. Nevertheless, technology had moved on and the stones would have been cut using pneumatic power tools and transported by horse-drawn wagons to the base of the tower for lifting. The building stones were drilled to take Lewis cramps (huge metal pincers which grip as they are lifted). Some of the drill marks can still be seen in the lower parts of the stonework, which is unusual on an architectural building of this date. Normally, you will only see such marks on utilitarian constructions, such as railway bridges or viaducts.

Although by 1861 £7,000 had been raised, two years later the work had come to a complete halt and the original contractor, Thomas Harvie of Hamilton, had been dismissed for underestimating the scale of the work at £5,262. There were even suggestions that the monument be left abandoned and the plant and machinery for its construction sold off. However, the fundraising went on and the tower continued to rise. The last stage of construction – the crown spire - was the most delicate and the most expensive in labour and materials. The crown spire was the most complex and dramatic element of the whole composition. In terms of construction the spire presented difficulties which the simple load-bearing masonry of the walls did not. In order to 'set' the arched construction it had to be built on a form, a timber armature which held the structure in place until it was complete and the capstone in place. Once complete, the form was struck (removed) and everyone held their breath until the structure settled safely.

◦ View from below of the monument's crown spire.

Since the monument was opened it has been modified to suit demand and necessity. The opening ceremony itself in 1869 when it was formally handed over to the Custodiers was a fairly low key affair. The Town Council of Stirling, who had agreed to take possession of the monument on its completion, leased it to a keeper. Originally the keeper's house and the tower were separated across an open courtyard but this was roofed over in glass in 1874 and became an entrance hall. Entry was free but visitors paid a charge of 2d to climb the narrow spiral staircase to the top. Having walked all the way up to the monument, the ascent to the tower was only for the fitter visitors, and not for crinolined women or girls who would wait below. With the money left over from building the monument and the revenue from teas and access to the tower there was £600 left for embellishment and for the keeper's salary.

WALLACE MONUMENT, STIRLING.

A souvenir paperweight, one of many objects produced due to the success of the monument as a Victorian visitor attraction.

Wooden pin cushion souvenir, with a view of the monument, late 19th century.

• A postcard of the monument, photographed 1890.

The monument was a huge success. Between 1869 and 1885 it attracted a yearly average of 12,600 visitors but it also attracted a great deal of architectural criticism. The finished work was decried by many architects and critics variously as 'a gigantic mistake' and a 'fantastic nightmare of a memorial'. But architectural fashions come and go and such a prominent building was bound to be a target for detractors. Once the fashion for this type of Scotch Baronial architecture had passed it was subjected to ever more hysterical critical abuse and the monument became a byword for the style's pretentiousness. The Glasgow and London architect J. J. Stevenson summed up the criticism in his influential publication *House Architecture* (1880) when he appealed for a calmer Scottish architectural inspiration:

'The enthusiasts for Scotch nationality have recently erected, as a monument to Wallace, a tower which alters, and some think destroys, the contour of a beautiful hill near Stirling. Corbelling has run mad in it, making marvellous protuberances where one does not expect them; corners are hacked out of it, and the pieces stuck on somewhere else. The design seems to aim at being wild.'

However, time has moved on and the National Wallace Monument is now one of Scotland's best loved buildings.

Crowds of visitors at the National Wallace Monument in the 1880s.
Stirling Smith Art Gallery & Museum.

35

The National Wallace Monument sits at the highest point of the Abbey Craig, 91.44 metres above sea level. Its total height is 67.06 metres and it is 10.97 metres square. The walls are 5.5 metres thick and reduce to a width of 1.5 metres at the wallhead. At the east side of the tower is the keeper's house, which was formerly rented to the custodian of the monument, who also ran a tea room and charged for entry to the upper floors. The sculpture immediately above the main doorway represents the arms of Sir William Wallace surmounted by a Scottish thistle. On the left is a straight staircase leading to an octagonal corner staircase on the north west angle, which climbs to the parapet below the crown spire. The staircase turret is pierced by open arrow slits. The ground floor of the tower originally contained a waiting room, and above was a Hall of Arms, the Hall of Heroes or 'Champion Room' and finally the Royal Chamber, containing Wallace's sword which had been ceremonially brought to the monument in 1885 from its historic resting place in Dumbarton Castle. The original scheme for the Royal Chamber was to ornament it with 'a series of brasses or shields in honour of all the Scottish kings since Wallace struggled'.

The halls are stone, arched and measure 7.32 metres square. At the top of the staircase's 246 steps, there is a massive parapet, 1.5 metres high and 0.5 metres thick. Above again on a raised platform protected by a low parapet of stone balls, is an open space, 7.9 metres square and paved with Craigmyllie stone from Arbroath. The apex of the monument is formed by a massive crown spire, 21.37 metres high and built of local freestone. The crown spire is composed of eight arms converging in a central point and locked together by a capstone.

The Wallace Sword on display in the National Wallace Monument.

The Wallace Sword has been venerated as a national icon since at least the time of James IV, who embellished its handle. The idea of a leader bearing a mighty sword gained currency from the 14th century. Although the sword is genuinely from the time of Wallace, it is unlikely to have been wielded by a man on horseback. The blade would have been swung or pointed primarily at the cavalry, killing the horse and bringing down the rider.

An original drawing produced by Rochead.

D. W. Stevenson

1842 - 1904

David Watson Stevenson was born at Ratho near Edinburgh in 1842. He was appointed to the Edinburgh sculptor William Brodie (1815 - 1881) and won a student prize for a version of the *Venus de Milo*. Like many aspiring artists he completed his studies by visiting Rome, the home of the classical sculpture on which 19th century work was based.

With Sir John Steell, Stevenson contributed figures to the Prince Albert Memorial in Charlotte Square, Edinburgh and also to the Scott Monument. He designed the statue of Hygeia inside the little neoclassical temple of St. Bernard's Well at the Water of Leith, Edinburgh. He also designed four figures for the ironfounder Walter Macfarlane's Saracen Fountain at the Glasgow International Exhibition of 1901 (later moved to Alexandra Park, Glasgow). Stevenson's other pieces include the understated memorial at Paisley Abbey Close to the poet and song-writer Robert Tannahill (1884), a statue of Burns at Leith and also one of his paramour Highland Mary (1896) at Dunoon. He formed a successful partnership with his younger brother William Grant Stevenson (1849 - 1919) who designed the gigantic Wallace bronze at Rosemount Viaduct, Aberdeen. Having got the original commission for the Wallace statue, Stevenson went on to carry out almost all of the commissions for the Hall of Heroes.

Stevenson's studio was in the artistic colony of Dean Village, Edinburgh, where he modelled the huge plaster for the Wallace statue.

Wallace Statue

Sculptor:	D. W. Stevenson
	4 metre bronze figure, 6.4 metres to the point of the uplifted sword
Donor:	Subscription funds
Unveiled:	25 June 1887 by the Marquess of Bute

The corbel on which the statue is placed is 15 metres from the ground. The three ton statue was lifted by crane by Messrs Burt and Shaw of Stirling. The figure was originally intended to be carried out in stone with the Wallace figure 'leaning on his two-handed sword'. The pose would have been similar to the Dryburgh monument.

⋅ The sculptor D. W. Stevenson with the plaster model of the Wallace statue.

Hall of Heroes

Most of the sculpture with which the monument was embellished is in the vaulted space on the second floor. The Hall of Heroes was designed to bring the 'heroic' up to date and to attract visitors and interest. It was the Scottish writer Thomas Carlyle who had made the idea of heroes and heroism popular for the 19th century. However, the idea of the hero was taken well beyond traditional notions of brave freedom fighters. It included heroes of 19th century endeavour and reform, and even the inventor of gas lighting, William Murdoch. The space contains 15 white marble busts and one bronze, donated at different times, sometimes by subscription and at other times by a single donor, such as Andrew Carnegie, the Scots-born billionaire philanthropist. The original idea was for busts of 'Burns, Sir Walter Scott, James Watt, Sir Ralph Abercromby, Sir John Moore, Lord Clyde, John Knox.' Of those suggested, Burns, Scott, John Knox and Watt were finally installed.

Although the executed busts are all of men, as we might expect at this date, Professor Masson in his speech at the unveiling of the bust of Carlyle on 25 July 1891 recommended two women for the Hall of Heroes: Lady Elizabeth Wardlaw (1677 - 1727), a poet, and Baroness Nairne (1766 - 1845), the prolific Scots song writer (*Bonnie Cherlie's Noo Awa, Caller Herrin*). This list of candidates remained open and more busts were expected to follow, but the last - of Sir David Brewster - was installed in 1907. The list below also includes the two busts, of Charles Rogers and William Burns, which were installed much later in the entrance hall created in 1874.

° Hall of Heroes.

KING ROBERT THE BRUCE

(1274 - 1329)

ROBERT BURNS

(1759 - 1796)

Scotland's national poet

DAVID LIVINGSTONE

(1813 - 1873)

Explorer and missionary

THOMAS CARLYLE

(1795 - 1881)

Author

ADAM SMITH

(1723 - 1790)

Economist

JAMES WATT

(1736 - 1819)

Inventor and engineer

ROBERT TANNAHILL

(1774 - 1810)

Poet and songwriter

SIR WALTER SCOTT

(1771 - 1832)

Poet and novelist

ALLAN RAMSAY

(1686 - 1758)

Poet

WILLIAM MURDOCH

(1754 - 1839)

Inventor and engineer

HUGH MILLER

(1802 - 1856)

Author and geologist

JOHN KNOX

(1505 - 1572)

Religious reformer

WILLIAM EWART GLADSTONE

(1809 - 1898)

Politician

THOMAS CHALMERS

(1780 - 1847)

Theologian and reformer

GEORGE BUCHANAN

(1506 - 1582)

Historian, dramatist and poet

SIR DAVID BREWSTER

(1781 - 1868)

Scientist

Stained glass

There are 11 stained glass windows in the monument, all carried out to a comprehensive scheme by the firm of James Ballantine and Son for the sum of £210. The ground floor has the Honours of Scotland (Scotland's crown jewels and symbols of nationhood discovered by Walter Scott in 1818 at Edinburgh Castle, where they had remained hidden in a chest for more than 100 years). These are flanked by unicorns bearing the Lion Rampant and the flag of Scotland, the Saltire Cross of St Andrew, patron saint of Scotland. The Hall of Arms (first floor) has the arms of Great Britain, Scotland, Wallace and the Burgh of Stirling. The Hall of Heroes has Wallace, Bruce, an archer and a spearman.

The firm of James Ballantine and Son was founded in Edinburgh in 1837. Ballantine's firm had established their credentials for this type of work by winning the contract for the armorial windows at the Scott Monument in 1834, however it was Ballantine's son Alexander who carried out the work at the National Wallace Monument.

· Stained glass window of a spearman.   · Stained glass window of Robert the Bruce.

Stained glass window of William Wallace. ·

The Abbey Craig

In terms of geology, the Abbey Craig is a basaltic 'crag and tail' rock, similar to those at both Stirling and Edinburgh Castles. Like these two it was also a place of strength that could be defended on three steep sides. Evidence of early settlement has been found on the lower slopes of the hill and it seems likely that Neolithic farmers cultivated the area, using the rock itself as a redoubt in times of trouble and also as a kind of early 'power centre' similar to the much later medieval castles. Below the Craig in the river plain the ground was difficult marshland, which, of course, added to the attractions of the site as a place of refuge. It is interesting that the site seems at this stage to have been preferred to Stirling Castle Rock which has, as yet, offered up no evidence of similar settlements. Remains of one of Scotland's earliest Iron Age forts exist at the Abbey Craig. The fort's solid defensive walls were created not by traditional building but by fusing or melting stones in a matrix of wooden posts which were then burned to form a 'vitrified' wall.

⁎ The classic 'crag and tail' profile of the Abbey Craig with the monument tower.

* Stirling Castle.

The focus of local power later shifted to Stirling Castle Rock where began the creation of the country's finest setpiece of medieval and Renaissance architecture. The Craig was left in peace and became a much-loved local resource but surged suddenly back into prominence when, in 1856, the decision to site the National Wallace Monument there was taken. According to tradition, Wallace and his forces had camped on the Abbey Craig on the night before the momentous Battle of Stirling Bridge in 1297. The Craig had also long been admired as a place of great scenic beauty and this was enriched forever by the National Wallace Monument. Today's visitors to the monument can enjoy the added attraction of waymarked nature trails on the Craig's beautiful wooded slopes.

* Edinburgh Castle.

Who subscribed to the monument?

The monument was built entirely by public subscription. An enthusiastic and influential Glasgow proponent was John McAdam, a well-known political reformer and supporter of European nationalist movements from Hungary to Poland. It was McAdam who persuaded Kossuth, the Hungarian nationalist, Garibaldi and Mazzini of Italy and the socialist reformers Karl Blind and Louis Blanc to 'subscribe' (McAdam contributed the money) and to write in praise of Wallace so that their handwritten letters could be displayed at the monument and thereby attract visitors. Garibaldi, who has been called 'the Wallace of Italy', had two paintings of Wallace in his bedroom. The letters duly arrived and were framed using timber from the Wallace Oak at Elderslie (one of many ancient trees which had, according to legend, sheltered Wallace) and displayed at the monument. They are now at Stirling Smith Museum and Art Gallery.

The rest of the subscribers to the National Wallace Monument came from all walks of life and all parts of the world, but the majority of the money was raised in Glasgow. J. T. Rochead, the eventual winner of the competition, had himself subscribed generously with the sum of £5-5-0 and the only other Glasgow architect to make such a contribution was James Smith. The amount was among the larger donations, matching even that of the wealthy Glasgow ironfounder William Connal. A few very large individual sums were also donated, including the huge sum of £1200 from Mr W. Drummond of Rockdale. An appeal office was set up in Glasgow and after a poor start a great deal of money flowed in, but the committee soon reported that the 'working classes' were not responding and arrangements for a 'special appeal' were soon made. Public meetings were held in many parts of the city and small donations from 'working men' were taken. It was in the nature of such a monument that the construction could be gradual and could continue as money came in.

Hall of Arms

Above the ground floor reception hall was originally the Hall of Arms. This space was used to display a collection of medieval and later weapons and suits of armour donated by a local collector, Mr McInnes, in 1885, and brought from the armoury of the Tower of London by the Secretary of State for War. This area was converted in 1995 into an audiovisual display of Wallace's life.

• Giuseppe Garibaldi (1807 - 1882). Portrait painted
onto glass, 1864, to commemorate his visit to Britain.
Stirling Smith Art Gallery & Museum.

• 'Wallace Oak' at Torwood. One of the many ancient trees associated with Wallace.
Stirling Smith Art Gallery & Museum.

• The framed letters were displayed to raise funds for the building of the monument.
Stirling Smith Art Gallery & Museum.

Acknowledgements

We would like to thank Elspeth King and the Stirling Smith Art Gallery & Museum for their help and assistance in the production of this book.

Images licensed through Scran (www.scran.ac.uk):
Stirling Smith Art Gallery & Museum: *p.2, p.4, p.8, p.10, p.12 (top), p.16 (bottom), p.24, p.28, p.30 (top), p.34 (background), p.35, p.44, p.47 (top right), p.47 (bottom)*
Paisley Art Gallery & Museum: *p.15*
Bob McCutcheon: *p.9 (right)*
National Trust for Scotland: *p.14, p.31 (bottom)*
Padeapix: *p.18 (left)*
St Andrews University Library: *p.18 (right), p.34 (left)*
University of Strathclyde: *p.19 (left)*
Glasgow City Libraries: *p.19 (top)*
Edinburgh City Libraries: *p.21*
Marius Alexander: *p.23 (top)*
University of Dundee: *p.29*
Glasgow University Library: *p.31 (top)*
National Museums of Scotland: *p.32 (left), p.34 (bottom right)*
Lammerburn Collection: *p.32 (right)*
Perth Museum and Art Gallery: *p.34 (top right)*
Scottish Media Group: *p.33*

Mary Evans Picture Library: *p.5 (top), p.5 (bottom), p.6 (bottom), p.7 (left), p.7 (right), p.9 (left), p.12 (bottom), p.19 (bottom right)*

Getty Images: *p.17 (right), p.20, p.22, p.23 (left), p.25 (top), p.25 (bottom)*

Scottish National Portrait Gallery: *p.7 (middle), p.13*

© Mark Churms.com. 1994. All rights reserved: *p.16 (top)*

Hungarian Museums: *p.17 (left)*

By courtesy of the Mitchell Library, Cultural & Leisure Services, Glasgow City Council: *p.30 (bottom)*

Scottish Viewpoint: *front cover, p.45 (top), p.45 (bottom), back inset page*

Photolibrary.com: *p.23 (bottom right)*

Crown Copyright: Royal Commission on the Ancient and Historical Monuments of Scotland: *p.26, p.38*

Argyll, the Isles, Loch Lomond, Stirling and the Trossachs Tourist Board: *p.1, p.3, p.27 (top right), p.27 (bottom right), p.39, p.40, p.42 (left), p.42 (right), p.43*

20th Century Fox: *p.6 (top)*

Stirling Smith Art Gallery & Museum: *p.47 (top left)*

Photography by Paul Zanre: *p.36, p.41*